1ST GRADE AMERICAN HISTORY
EARLY PILGRIMS OF AMERICA

BABY PROFESSOR
EDUCATION KIDS

Speedy Publishing LLC
40 E. Main St. #1156
Newark, DE 19711
www.speedypublishing.com

The Pilgrims left because they were tired of the Government telling them what to believe and how to live.

The Pilgrims were a group of English settlers who left Europe in search of religious freedom in the Americas. They founded the Plymouth Colony in 1620.

A Pilgrim is someone who travels for religious reasons.

They were called "Separatists" because they wanted to separate from the Church of England and worship God in their own way.

The Pilgrims left for the New World on August 15, 1620. The Pilgrims originally set sail with two ships; the Speedwell and the Mayflower.

The Speedwell started to leak and had to return to port. The Mayflower managed to fit 102 total passengers.

The Pilgrims were finally successful in sailing on September 16, 1620.

The voyage across the Atlantic Ocean was long and difficult. They ran out of fresh water and many people became sick.

The Pilgrims didn't reach the new world until November 9, 1620.

The Pilgrims signed a document that is today called the Mayflower Compact.

The compact declared that the colonists were loyal to the King of England, that they were Christians who served God, that they would make fair and just laws, and that they would each work for the good of the colony.

The Pilgrims searched for a good place to build a settlement. They eventually found a location called Plymouth.

By the fall of 1621, only half of the pilgrims survived. The survivors, thankful to be alive, decided to prepare a thanksgiving feast.

In the Pilgrim household, the adults sat down to dinner and the children waited on them.

The first Thanksgiving celebration in the fall of 1621 went on for three days.

CPSIA information can be obtained
at www.ICGtesting.com
Printed in the USA
LVHW060113290420
654695LV00017B/2843

9 781682 601730